Extreme Animals

Nature's Best Jumpers

Frankie Stout

PowerKiDS press
New York

For Nicholas Anthony Lazarus, a wonderful nephew

Published in 2008 by The Rosen Publishing Group, Inc.
29 East 21st Street, New York, NY 10010

Copyright © 2008 by The Rosen Publishing Group, Inc.

All rights reserved. No part of this book may be reproduced in any form without permission in writing from the publisher, except by a reviewer.

First Edition

Editor: Jennifer Way
Book Design: Greg Tucker
Photo Researcher: Nicole Pristash

Photo Credits: Cover, p. 9 © Jozsef Szentpeteri; pp. 5, 7, 11, 15, 17 (inset), 17 (main), 19, 21 Shutterstock.com; pp. 12–13 © BIOS Chatagnon Jean-Paul/Peter Arnold, Inc.

Library of Congress Cataloging-in-Publication Data

Stout, Frankie.
  Nature's best jumpers / Frankie Stout. — 1st ed.
    p. cm. — (Extreme animals)
  Includes index.
  ISBN 978-1-4042-4155-8 (lib. bdg.)
  1. Animal jumping—Juvenile literature. I. Title.
  QP310.J86S76 2008
  573.7'9—dc22
                                              2007022951

Manufactured in the United States of America

Contents

Extreme Jumpers	4
Up, Down, and All Around	6
These Legs Are Made for Jumping	8
Large Leaping Cats	10
The Cougar	12
Jumping Spiders	14
The Smallest Super Jumpers	16
Jumping Bugs	18
All Jumpers, Big and Small	20
Jumping Facts	22
Glossary	23
Index	24
Web Sites	24

Extreme Jumpers

Some animals are known as great jumpers. They can jump up very high or across long distances.

These **extreme** jumpers come in all sizes and shapes and live in all kinds of **habitats**. Frogs, rabbits, kangaroos, cougars, spiders, and many other types of creatures are known for their jumping skills. Some **insects**, like fleas and froghoppers, can jump distances that might not be far in inches (cm) but that are many times the size of their own body. From the smallest bug to the furriest cat, extreme jumpers are some of the coolest animals in the world.

Kangaroos have very large feet and springy back legs that help them jump. Kangaroos also use their fat tail to help keep their balance.

Up, Down, and All Around

Animals use their legs to jump. Many extreme jumpers have legs and feet that are **adapted** for jumping. Powerful leg **muscles** help an animal take off into the air very quickly or very high.

Some jumpers, like frogs, use only their back legs to jump and then land on all four legs. Other animals, like rabbits, use both their front and their back legs to jump around. Still other animals, like grasshoppers, jump and land only on their back legs.

You can see the grasshopper's powerful back legs in this picture. A grasshopper can jump nearly 3 feet (1 m). That is about 80 times the length of its body!

These Legs Are Made for Jumping

Frogs are good jumpers. Most frogs live on the ground and get around by jumping. Frogs' back legs have big muscles that make jumping easy. Their big feet help them push off the ground with a lot of force. As a frog leaps, its back legs reach out to full length. Frogs' back legs are almost twice as long as their front legs!

Frogs' front legs touch down first and help soften the landing after a big jump. By the time a frog lands on its front legs, its back legs will be folded at its knees and ready to jump again right away.

Here you can see a frog giving itself a big push with its back legs as it jumps. Most frogs can jump around 10 times the length of their body. That is like a 6-foot (1.8 m) person jumping 60 feet (18 m)!

Large Leaping Cats

Another well-known jumper is the cougar. The cougar is a large cat that lives in the wild. Cougars are also called mountain lions, pumas, or catamounts.

Cougars are carnivores. This means that they eat meat. They like to live in places where there are lots of animals to hunt.

When they are hunting, cougars will follow their **prey** quietly through trees and brush. They will get close and then leap onto the prey's back and kill the prey quickly. Cougars are great leapers and excellent hunters. They can jump about 18 feet (5.5 m) up into a tree and as far as 20 feet (6 m) on the ground!

Cougars are part of a group of animals known as the big cats. Other big cats are lions, tigers, leopards, jaguars, and cheetahs.

The Cougar

Strong leg muscles allow a cougar to make its 20-foot (6 m) jumps.

Cougars measure about 6 ½ feet (2 m) from the head to the tip of their tail.

Picky Eaters

A cougar will almost never feed on an animal that it did not kill.

12

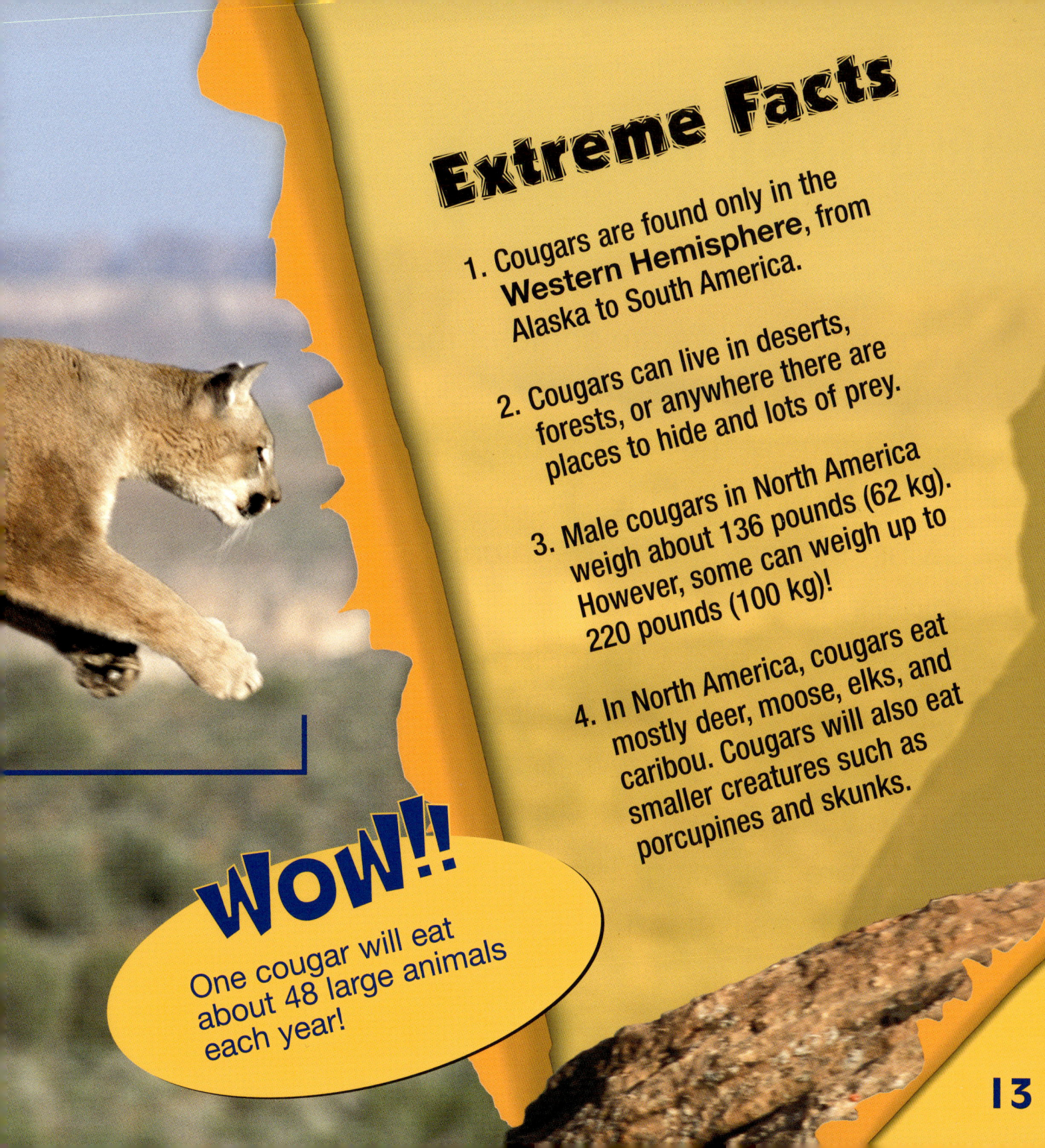

Extreme Facts

1. Cougars are found only in the **Western Hemisphere**, from Alaska to South America.

2. Cougars can live in deserts, forests, or anywhere there are places to hide and lots of prey.

3. Male cougars in North America weigh about 136 pounds (62 kg). However, some can weigh up to 220 pounds (100 kg)!

4. In North America, cougars eat mostly deer, moose, elks, and caribou. Cougars will also eat smaller creatures such as porcupines and skunks.

Wow!!
One cougar will eat about 48 large animals each year!

Jumping Spiders

Jumping spiders are some of the smallest big jumpers. They measure only about .12 to .67 inch (3–17 mm) yet they can jump distances of 10 to 50 times the length of their body!

Most spiders spin webs to catch their prey. Jumping spiders use their extreme jumping skills to **pounce** on theirs and catch it with their mouth. To see their prey from far away, jumping spiders have excellent eyesight with their eight eyes. When a jumping spider sees a bug it wants to catch, it will leave behind a thread of silk before pouncing. That way the spider can climb back up the silk if it misses its prey.

There are around 500 different kinds of jumping spiders. There are jumping spiders just about everywhere in the world.

15

The Smallest Super Jumpers

Fleas are super jumpers for their small size. They are around 1/16 to 1/8 inch (2–3 mm) long. They can jump a distance of about 13 inches (33 cm), which is up to 200 times the length of their body!

Fleas and other jumping insects have something called resilin inside them. Resilin is springy. The muscles in a flea's legs can store **energy** for jumping in the resilin.

This skill makes the flea the best jumper for its size. A person who had the jumping ability of a flea could jump about 1,200 feet (366 m)! That is the size of four football fields.

The world record for a person jumping from a standing position is about 12 feet (4 m), or two times the body length of a 6-foot (1.8 m) person. *Inset:* A flea's jump of 13 inches (33 cm) is hundreds of times the length of its body.

17

Jumping Bugs

Many insects get around by jumping. Some, like grasshoppers and crickets, use their long legs to power their jumps. Those with short legs, like froghoppers, store muscle energy in their body to shoot themselves into the air, much like an arrow.

Froghoppers, also known as spittlebugs, are only about .2 inch (5 mm) long. Some froghoppers can jump about 28 inches (71 cm) into the air. That is the highest that any insect is known to jump.

The froghopper is the world's highest-jumping insect. It can jump two times as high as a flea. These insects are known as spittlebugs because the stuff their body makes to hide them looks like spit.

All Jumpers, Big and Small

All kinds of animals, including people, use their body to jump and leap around in their habitats. Jumping may help one animal catch its food for the week, and it may help another animal escape being eaten.

Jumping can be a great way of getting around, for both big and small animals. Extreme jumpers have a body that has adapted for jumping great heights or distances. This helps extreme jumpers **survive** in the wild.

Dolphins can jump about 16 feet (5 m) out of the water. There are many reasons that dolphins might jump. One reason may be that they can move faster through the air than through the water.

Jumping Facts

Highest Jump: A cougar can jump up to 18 feet (5.5 m).

Biggest Jump for Smallest Creature: A flea can jump up to 200 times its body size.

Longest Jump for Insects: Spittlebugs can jump about 28 inches (71 cm).

Longest Jump by a Frog: 21 feet (6.4 m).

Weirdest Jumper: Mexican jumping beans have small insects inside them. As the insects move around in the bean, the bean looks like it is jumping.

Scaliest Jumper: Flying fish do not really fly. They jump out of the water and **glide** for hundreds of feet (m) through the air!

Glossary

adapted (uh-DAPT-ed) Changed to fit requirements.

energy (EH-nur-jee) The power to work or to act.

extreme (ik-STREEM) Going past the expected or common.

glide (GLYD) To fall freely through the air without flying.

habitats (HA-beh-tats) The kinds of land where animals or plants naturally live.

insects (IN-sekts) Small creatures that often have six legs and wings.

muscles (MUH-sulz) Parts of the body that make the body move.

pounce (POWNS) To creep up and jump on something by surprise.

prey (PRAY) An animal that is hunted by another animal for food.

survive (sur-VYV) To live longer than, to stay alive.

Western Hemisphere (WES-tern HEH-muh-sfeer) The western half of Earth.

Index

B
body, 4, 14, 16, 18, 20
bug, 4, 14

C
cat, 4, 10
cougar(s), 4, 10, 12–13, 22
creature(s), 4, 13, 22

D
distance(s), 4, 14, 16, 20

E
energy, 16, 18

F
flea(s), 4, 16, 22

froghoppers, 4, 18
frog(s), 4, 6, 8, 22

H
habitats, 4, 20

I
insects, 4, 16, 18, 22

L
legs, 6, 8, 16, 18

M
muscles, 6, 8, 16

P
prey, 10, 13–14

R
rabbits, 4, 6

S
size(s), 4, 16, 22
skill(s), 4, 14, 16
spiders, 4, 14

T
types, 4

W
water, 22
Western Hemisphere, 13
wild, 10, 20
world, 4

Web Sites

Due to the changing nature of Internet links, PowerKids Press has developed an online list of Web sites related to the subject of this book. This site is updated regularly. Please use this link to access the list:
www.powerkidslinks.com/exan/jump/